THE SPIRIT OF PROPHECY

YOU HOLD THE KEYS!

MORRIS CERULLO

Unless otherwise noted, all Scripture references are from the
King James version of the Bible.

Scripture references marked TAB are from The Amplified Bible
version Copyright © 1965 by Zondervan Publishing House.

Scripture references marked NIV are from the New
International version of the Bible, Copyright © 1973,1978,1984,
by the International Bible Society.

Scripture references marked NAS are from the
New American Standard version of the Bible. Copyright ©
1960,1962,1963, 1968, 1971,1972,1975, 1977
by the Lockman Foundation.

Scripture references marked TLB are from the Living Bible.
Copyright © 1971 by Tyndale House Publishers,
Wheaton, Illinois 60187. All rights reserved.

Published by Morris Cerullo World Evangelism
Copyright © 1999 San Diego, California
Printed in the United States of America

Morris Cerullo World Evangelism
P.O. Box 85277 San Diego, CA 92186-5277

Morris Cerullo World Evangelism of Canada
P.O. Box 3600 Concord, Ontario L4K1B6

Morris Cerullo World Evangelism
P.O. Box 277, Hemel Hempstead, HERTS HP2 7DH

Tel: (858) 277-2200
Web: www.morriscerullo.com
E-mail: morris cerullo@mcwe.com

Cover artwork has been used by permission.
It is from a series of illustrations by
Pat Marvenko Smith ©1982, 1992 on the Book of Revelation,
available as art prints and visual teaching aids.
A free brochure is available from
Revelation Productions 1-800-327-7330
Website: www.revelationillustrated.com

TABLE OF CONTENTS

INTRODUCTION

We are living in the opening days of a new millennium. With the advent of the year 2000, people everywhere are more conscious of, and more concerned about, the future...

...What lies ahead for this world?

...What does the future hold for me as a child of God?

...How can I properly prepare to face the future?

Maybe you have pondered some of these questions yourself in recent days.

The good news is that you do not have to be fearful about the future. Why? Because God has a divine plan He is working out in this world. Nothing can alter it. You just need to know it. Nothing can abort it. You do not have to be confused about the future because God is now placing in your hands the keys to understanding biblical prophecy – the most glorious book in the world – the Book of Revelation.

Your response may be, "Who? Me? I have never understood prophecy."

Yes...I mean YOU! You already have in your possession the start to unfold keys to understanding biblical prophecy. All you must do is learn how to use these keys – and that is the purpose of Volume One and the eleven others that follow in my new millennium 2000 prophecy series.

If you seriously apply yourself to this study, you will never again be confused by prophecy. You will know the events before they happen.

Jesus declared to Peter:

> *And I will give unto thee the keys of the kingdom of heaven: and whatsoever thou shalt bind on earth shall be*

bound in heaven: and whatsoever thou shalt loose on
earth shall be loosed in heaven. (Matthew 16:19)

The keys to the kingdom were first put into Peter's hands because he was called by God to open the door of faith to the Gentiles (Acts 10:28). But these spiritual keys were not reserved exclusively for him. They are delegated to all of God's people – and that is why you need to know what they are and how to use them.

Quite simply, keys are used to open doors that are locked. This is true in the natural world and it is true also in the spiritual world. God has given us supernatural keys to open doors of spiritual revelation.

Note that Jesus refers to "keys" – meaning more than one and that they are specific keys – "to the kingdom of heaven." Related references reveal that these spiritual keys were given to us for three major purposes:

1. The keys to the kingdom of heaven give us command over the enemy, Satan – We have the authority to bind and loose spiritual powers in both heaven and earth:

> *And I will give unto thee the keys of the kingdom of heaven: and whatsoever thou shalt bind on earth shall be bound in heaven: and whatsoever thou shalt loose on earth shall be loosed in heaven. (Matthew 16:19)*

2. These keys authorize us to exercise discipline and order in the kingdom of God – we have the power to admit people to the kingdom:

> *And Jesus came and spake unto them, saying, All power is given unto me in heaven and in eaerth. Go ye therefore, and teach all nations, baptizing them in the name of the Father, and of the Son, and of the Holy Ghost: Teaching them to observe all things whatsoever i have commanded you: and, lo, I am with you always, even unto the end of the world. Amen. (Matthew 28:18-20, KJV)*

We have the power to expel those who walk contrary to the Word:

> *It is reported commonly that there is fornication among you, and such fornication as is not so much as named among the Gentiles, that one should have his father's wife...In the name of our Lord Jesus Christ, when ye are gathered together, and my spirit, with the power of our Lord Jesus Christ, To deliver such an one unto Satan for the destruction of the flesh, that the spirit may be saved in the day of the Lord Jesus. (1 Corinthians 5:1,4-5)*

We have the power to restore those who have truly repented:

> *Sufficient to such a man is this punishment, which was inflicted of many. So that contrariwise ye ought rather to forgive him, and comfort him, lest perhaps such a one should be swallowed up with overmuch sorrow. (2 Corinthians 2:6-7)*

3. The keys to the kingdom give us the ability to open or shut the door to the knowledge of the kingdom of God:

> *Woe unto you, lawyers! For ye have taken away the key of knowledge: ye entered not in yourselves, and them that were entering in ye hindered. (Luke 11:52)*

This means that you already have in your hands the keys to knowledge in God's kingdom! All you must do is learn to use them...
...and that is the purpose of the new millennium prophecy series. With Volume One, we are starting an exciting spiritual journey into the future as we study together the prophetic Book of Revelation.

Notice that I didn't say we are making a "theological" trip. We are making a "spiritual" journey. On the island of *Patmos,* Apostle John didn't receive a dry, dead, theological explanation of future events. He received a powerful, dynamic, life-changing prophetic revelation. He received a revelation of Christ in all His Glory, he saw into the throne room of Heaven, and he received a supernatural unveiling of God's end-time plan. It was so awesome that John actually fell down as though he were dead:

And when I saw him, I fell at his feet as dead. And he laid his right hand upon me, saying unto me, Fear not; I am the first and the last. (Revelation 1:17)

INTRODUCTION

THE SPIRIT OF PROPHECY

John was *"in the Spirit"* when he received this revelation from God:

> *I was in the Spirit on the Lord's day, and heard behind*
> *me a great voice, as of a trumpet...(Revelation 1:10)*

The only way you can receive this revelation is to receive it into your spirit. You must go beyond head knowledge. You must allow the Word of God to penetrate your spirit – down deep inside your inner man – and then it will become alive to you. Then you will be filled with excitement and awe instead of apprehension and dread concerning the things which are occurring and will soon occur.

The Apostle John was given a supernatural revelation which included sights and sounds he had never known before in the natural world. It was difficult for him to describe the experience in terms that people of that day (and our day) would understand. Some of the things he saw were symbolic, others were literal.

You must not attempt to understand the Book of Revelation with your natural mind. You cannot interpret biblical prophecy that way. It won't work. God's end-time plan was unveiled to His servant, John, while he was in the Spirit. You must receive this understanding by the Spirit of God. Jesus said:

> *He that hath an ear, let him hear what the Spirit*
> *saith unto the churches; To him that overcometh will I*
> *give to eat of the tree of life, which is in the midst of the*
> *paradise of God. (Revelation 2:7)*

Jesus was not referring to our natural ears. He was referring to our spiritual ears. The Apostle Paul declared:

> *But as it is written, Eye hath not seen, nor ear*
> *heard, neither have entered into the heart of man, the*

*things which God hath prepared for them that love
him. But God hath revealed them unto us by his Spirit:
for the Spirit searcheth all things, yea, the deep things
of God. (1 Corinthians 2:9-10)*

Over the years, there has been much confusion and division in
the Church regarding the Book of Revelation. Bible scholars who
have studied this book for years have depended upon their
natural reasoning to interpret the Scriptures or simply rehashed
other men's theories. Theologians have set forth so many
different speculations and interpretations that many Christians
don't know what to believe. One week, they hear a preacher
declare one thing and the next week they hear someone else say
exactly the opposite.

Many believers avoid the Book of Revelation because they
think it is too complicated, too full of symbolism, and beyond
their understanding – but you already hold the keys to
knowledge of God's kingdom and I am going to show you how
to use them! When you complete this new millennium prophecy
series, you will no longer be confused about the future.

YOU WILL KNOW THAT YOU KNOW!

God has placed His Spirit within us so that we can know the
things He has given us:

*Now we have received, not the spirit of the world, but
the spirit which is of God; that we might know the things
that are freely given to us of God. (1 Corinthians 2:12)*

God has given us the Holy Spirit to show us things to come:

*Howbeit when he, the Spirit of truth, is come, he
will guide you into all truth: for he shall not speak of
himself; but whatsoever he shall hear, that shall he speak:
and he will shew you things to come. (John 16:13)*

But the anointing which ye have received of him abideth in you,
and ye need not that any man teach you: but as the same anointing
teacheth you of all things, and is truth, and is no lie, and even as it
hath taught you, ye shall abide in him. (1 John 2:27)

THE IMPORTANCE OF
THE BOOK OF REVELATION

There are five major reasons it is important for believers to study the Book of Revelation:

1. You receive a blessing when you study it:

> *Blessed is he that readeth, and they that hear the words of this prophecy, and keep those things which are written therein: for the time is at hand. (Revelation 1:3)*

> *Behold, I come quickly: blessed is he that keepeth the sayings of the prophecy of this book. (Revelation 22:7)*

2. It is necessary for full maturity, as it is part of the Word:

> *All scripture is given by inspiration of God, and is profitable for doctrine, for reproof, for correction, for instruction in righteousness: That the man of God may be perfect, throughly furnished unto all good works. (2 Timothy 3:16-17)*

3. It enables you to understand the future and how it relates to the past and present:

> *The Revelation of Jesus Christ, which God gave unto him, to shew unto his servants things which must shortly come to pass; and he sent and signified it by his angel unto his servant John. (Revelation 1:1)*

4. Prophecy authenticates the Word of God. Fulfilled prophecy authenticates that which the Word says is true:

> *...but prophesying serveth not for them that believe not, but for them which believe. (1 Corinthians 14:22)*

5. Prophecy affects the way we live. The advent of the end times motivates us to live holy lives, knowing that we will give an account of all things:

> *Seeing then that all these things shall be dissolved, what manner of persons ought ye to be in all holy conversation and godliness. (2 Peter 3:11)*

It motivates us to reach out to a lost and dying world when we realize that time is short:

> *I must work the works of him that sent me, while it is day: the night cometh, when no man can work. (John 9:4)*

From the beginning of time, God has had a master plan for the world:

> *(He) planned for the maturity of the times and the climax of the ages to unify all things and head them up and consummate them in Christ (both) things in heaven and things on earth. (Ephesians 1:10, TAB)*

The events that are happening on the earth today and those that will occur in the future are not by chance. They were designed from the beginning of time by a God of purpose, design, and objectivity and the details were recorded in His Word so His people could know the future, their ultimate destiny, and their part in His plan.

As you begin this study, I want you to open your spirit to God. Ask Him to speak to you personally concerning what He wants you to hear with your spiritual ears, to show you things in your life you need to see, and reveal to you what you must do to prepare for His coming.

God's purpose for revealing His end-time plan in the Book of Revelation is so that you can know what will happen in the future so you can be...

...Busy working the works of God (Matthew 25:14-30).

...Watching for the coming of Christ (Matthew 24:36-44).

...Prepared for the future (Matthew 15:1-13).

I believe God wants to accomplish four major things in your life through this prophetic series based upon the Book of Revelation.

YOU WILL learn how to accurately interpret biblical prophecy by using the keys to the kingdom God has placed in your hands.

YOU WILL be prepared to face the future from a position of knowing. You will no longer be confused, fearful, or doubting.

YOU WILL be able to face every negative circumstance you may encounter in the future with power and authority because you will know your destiny as a 100% conquering, victorious child of God.

YOU WILL rise up in these end times to take your God-given position of power, authority and dominion as we reap together the greatest spiritual harvest this world has ever witnessed.

Now you may be thinking, "Brother Cerullo, I've tried to understand prophecy before, but it was too confusing. Is it really possible for me to know God's end-time plan?"

Yes! Trust me! It is not only possible, but God WANTS you to have this revelation. That is why He gave it. That is why He had his servant, John, record it in His Word. A revelation is to reveal something, not to conceal it.

Jesus is coming soon! The time is at hand! It is time for us to understand the signs of the time, to watch, prepare, and be ready. It is time to use the keys God has given us to unlock the door to the future. Journey with me now to be embraced by the Spirit of Prophecy.

YOU HOLD THE KEYS!

The Isle of Patmos lies about thirty-seven miles west-southwest of Miletus in the Mediterranean Sea. It is about ten miles long and six miles wide at the north end, and consists mainly of volcanic hills and rocky ground. It was an island used by the Romans to exile prisoners.

It was in the year 95 A.D. during the reign of the Roman Emperor Domitian that the Apostle John was exiled here for his faith in God. This was no tropical paradise. It was a lonely, deserted, barren place. But it was the Lord's day and despite the fact John was alone and in desperate circumstances, he decided to worship God.

Little did John realize that this worship experience would not only dramatically transform his own life, it would impact generations to come and affect the destiny of the entire world. As John was in the Spirit on this Lord's day, he received...

> ...*The Revelation of Jesus Christ, which God gave unto him, to shew unto his servants things which must shortly come to pass; and he sent and signified it by his angel unto his servant John. (Revelation 1:1-2)*

The Book of Revelation begins with a bold declaration of its supernatural, divine authorship. God is its source. The word *"revelation"* used here is translated from the Greek word *"apokalupsis"* which means "an uncovering," or "drawing away of the veil of darkness." The revelation John received on the Isle of Patmos did not come through his natural mind, but it was revealed to him while he was "in the spirit." Four times in the Book of Revelation John is said to be "in the spirit": Revelation 1:9-10; 4:1-2; 17:1-3; and 21:9-10.

Spiritual revelation is not a function of the natural mind because our natural minds do not understand the things of the Spirit:

> *But the natural man receiveth not the things of the Spirit of God; for they are foolishness unto him: neither can he know them, because they are spiritually discerned. (1 Corinthians 2:14)*

That is why we must understand this revelation with our spiritual minds.

John received *"the Revelation of Jesus Christ, which God gave unto him."* Here is the divine order of transmission: God gave the revelation to Jesus and it was sent and signified (made known) to His servant, the Apostle John (Revelation 1:1, 4, 9; 22:8).

The purpose of this revelation was *"to shew unto his servants things which must shortly come to pass"* (Revelation 1:1-2) – it was given so that His people would know what will happen in the future.

This powerful Revelation came to John in one of the darkest times of his life. Divine revelation often comes in difficult times:

It was in exile that Jacob saw God at Bethel. (Genesis 35:1)

It was in exile that Moses met God at the burning bush. (Exodus 3:1-2)

It was in exile that Elijah heard the voice of God. (1 Kings 19:3-9)

It was in exile that Ezekiel saw the glory of the Lord. (Ezekiel 1:3)

It was in exile that Daniel saw his vision of God. (Daniel 7:9)

If you are going through a difficult time in your life you can either succumb to depression or pity, or you – like the Apostle John – can get in the spirit and begin to worship God.

Reflect for a moment: What might God be trying to birth through you or reveal to you in your darkest hour?

THE REVELATION OF JESUS CHRIST

We learn in this passage that the Book of Revelation is the *"revelation of Jesus Christ."* This book reveals more about Jesus Christ than any other book in the Bible. (Please take time to look up each of these references in the Book of Revelation.) Jesus is described as:

- Jesus Christ: 1:1
- Faithful witness: 1:5
- First begotten of the dead: 1:5
- Prince of kings of the earth: 1:5
- Alpha and Omega: 1:8
- First and the last: 1:17
- Son of man: 1:13
- Son of God: 2:18
- Keeper of David's keys: 3:7
- Keeper of keys of hell and death: 1:18
- Lion of Judah: 5:5
- Root of David: 5:5
- Slain Lamb: 5:6
- Angry Lamb: 6:16-17
- Tender Lamb: 7:17
- Our Lord: 11:8
- King of saints: 15:3
- Faithful and true: 19:11
- Word of God: 19:13
- King of kings: 19:16
- Lord of lords: 19:16
- Beginning and the end: 22:13
- Bright and morning star: 22:16

The key to understanding the Book of Revelation is to realize that it is a revelation about Jesus Christ.

Revelation 19:10 declares, *"for the testimony of Jesus is the spirit of prophecy."* This is a tremendous spiritual key to understanding prophecy, the entire Word of God, and the Living Word – Jesus Christ.

When Christ's disciples were walking the Emmaus Road and puzzling over things Christ had told them, Jesus supernaturally appeared to them and said, *"What manner of communications are these that ye have one to another, as ye walk, and are sad?"* (Luke 24:17). The disciples recounted to Him the recent events in Jerusalem, including the death of Jesus and the empty tomb discovered by the women three days later. Then Jesus said to them:

> *O fools, and slow of heart to believe all that the prophets have spoken: Ought not Christ to have suffered these things, and to enter into his glory? And beginning at Moses and all the prophets, he expounded unto them in all the scriptures the things concerning himself. (Luke 24:25-27)*

This passage is not only the key to prophecy, it is the key for understanding and interpreting the entire Word of God. Beginning with Moses and the Old Testament prophets right through to the Book of Revelation, all of the Scriptures concern the revelation of Jesus Christ and God's plan of the ages as fulfilled through Him.

A SEVENFOLD BLESSING

The first of a sevenfold blessing is pronounced in Revelation 1:3 and expanded in the remainder of the book. As a child of God, each of these blessings are yours to claim:

1. A blessing is pronounced upon those who read, hear, and keep those things written in the Book of Revelation:

> *Blessed is he that readeth, and they that hear the words of this prophecy, and keep those things which are written therein: for the time is at hand. (Revelation 1:3)*

This is why it is important for God's people to study and understand this Revelation.

2. A blessing is pronounced upon those who die in the Lord:

> *And I heard a voice from heaven saying unto me, Write, Blessed are the dead which die in the Lord from henceforth: Yea, saith the Spirit, that they may rest from their labours; and their works do follow them. (Revelation 14:13)*

3. A blessing is pronounced upon those who are spiritually diligent in keeping themselves from sin:

> *Behold, I come as a thief. Blessed is he that watcheth and keepeth his garments, lest he walk naked, and they see his shame. (Revelation 16:15)*

4. A blessing is pronounced on those who partake of the marriage supper of the lamb:

> *And he saith unto me, Write, Blessed are they which are called unto the marriage supper of the Lamb. (Revelation 19:9)*

5. **Those who are part of the first resurrection of the righteous are blessed (1 Thessalonians 4:17):**

> *Blessed and holy is he that hath part in the first resurrection: on such the second death hath no power, but they shall be priests of God and of Christ, and shall reign with him a thousand years. (Revelation 20:6)*

6. **Those who keep the words of this prophecy – who hold fast these truths and warnings – are blessed:**

> *Behold, I come quickly: Blessed is he that keepeth the sayings of the prophecy of this book. (Revelation 22:7)*

7. **God's blessings are upon those who do His commandments – those who conform their lives to His Word:**

> *Blessed are they that do his commandments, that they may have right to the tree of life, and may enter in through the gates into the city. (Revelation 22:14)*

A VICTORIOUS CHURCH

John opens the Book of Revelation by greeting and extending God's grace and peace to the seven churches which were in Asia:

> *John to the seven churches which are in Asia: Grace be unto you, and peace, from him which is, and which was, and which is to come; and from the seven Spirits which are before his throne; And from Jesus Christ, who is the faithful witness, and the first begotten of the dead, and the prince of the kings of the earth. Unto him that loved us, and washed us from our sins in his own blood, And hath made us kings and priests unto God and his Father; to him be glory and dominion for ever and ever. Amen. (Revelation 1:4-6)*

The major theme of Revelation is to present God's people as a victorious church. The "seven Spirits which are before His throne" refer to the Holy Spirit in the fullness of His ministry in the world and in the Church.

In Revelation 1:11, John was instructed to write down all that was revealed to him by the Spirit and send it to the seven churches in Asia. These seven churches – Ephesus, Smyrna, Pergamos, Thyatira, Sardis, Philadelphia and Laodicea – were located in the western part of Asia Minor. The revelations contained in this prophecy were given not only to comfort, strengthen, and encourage believers in the first century A.D. who were going through severe persecution, but also to reveal the great final victory God has planned for us, to prepare us for Christ's coming, and to strengthen believers down through the centuries.

It is evident that the message, warnings, and admonitions contained in this book are not only for the Early Church but are also meant for the entire Church throughout the centuries. The major theme of Revelation is Christ's victory, and that of His Church, over Satan – especially in the end times:

Jesus is revealed as the Victor and Conqueror over death, hell, the Antichrist, the false prophet, and all those who worship the Antichrist.

The Church is described as victorious, overcoming the power of Satan, *"by the blood of the Lamb and the word of their testimony."*

The triumphant Church is gathered out of all nations and we see it standing united before the Throne and before the Lamb.

The Church rules and reigns with Christ upon the earth for a thousand years.

THE REVELATION OF CHRIST

In John's opening salutation to the seven churches in Asia, he describes Christ as...

1. **The faithful witness. Jesus bore witness to the truth from God: He said,** *"To this end was I born, and for this cause came I into the world, that I should bear witness unto the truth..."* (John 18:37). **The Greek word for witness is** *"martyrs"* **which means "one who suffers death for allegiance to a cause." Christ is presented here, in verse five, as a model of how to endure – faithful to the truth even unto death (Colossians 1:18).**

2. **The firstborn of the dead. As the risen Christ with victory over death – the** *"firstborn of the dead"* **– He is exalted as the head over the Church and is given a position of authority over all things.** *"And he is the head of the body, the church: who is the beginning, the firstborn from the dead; that in all things he might have the preeminence"* **(Colossians 1:18).**

3. **The prince of the kings of the earth. Because of Christ's faithful witness and His victory over Satan and death, He now has a victorious position of supreme power and authority:** *"Far above all principality, and power, and might, and dominion, and every name that is named, not only in this world, but also in that which is to come"* **(Ephesians 1:21).**

John used these three titles to encourage the believers who were facing persecution and possible death to remain faithful as Christ was faithful, and in so doing they would also be victorious as He was victorious.

This is how John saw Jesus. How do you see Him? When you are faced with difficulties and trials, do you see Him as a faithful witness? Do you rely on His Word to see you through? Do you see Him in a position of power and authority over every circumstance in your life?

John also describes Jesus as the One who...

1. Loved us.
2. Has washed our sins from us with His own blood.
3. Has made us kings and priests unto God and His Father.

The word *"kings"* speaks of authority and the word *"priests"* means that we have open access into God's presence at any time.

How do you see yourself? Do you see yourself as weak, struggling, and unable to overcome? Or do you see yourself as greatly loved, a king and priest with access into the throne room of God?

JESUS IS COMING!

Right at the beginning of Revelation, John gives us the divine promise of Christ's return to earth:

> *Behold, he cometh with clouds; and every eye shall see him, and they also which pierced him: and all kindreds of the earth shall wail because of him. Even so, Amen. (Revelation 1:7)*

This truth is the great hope and expectation of all true believers today and it is the theme of Revelation. The death and resurrection of Christ and the promise of His second coming are the foundation of our hope. They were a great source of strength to the Early Church and are even more so to us today as we move into the final days of time before Christ's return.

This verse reveals how Jesus will return. He will come in the same manner in which He ascended into heaven:

> *And when he had spoken these things, while they beheld, he was taken up; and a cloud received him out of their sight. (Acts 1:9)*

As the disciples gazed into the heavens where Christ had gone, two angels announced that He would return in the same way He had ascended. They said:

> *Ye men of Galilee, why stand ye gazing up into heaven? This same Jesus, which is taken up from you into heaven, shall so come in like manner as ye have seen him go into heaven. (Acts 1: 11)*

This reminded them of what Jesus had taught them, revealing that...

> *Immediately after the tribulation of those days*
> *shall the sun be darkened, and the moon shall not give*
> *her light, and the stars shall fall from heaven, and the*
> *powers of the heavens shall be shaken: And then shall*
> *appear the sign of the Son of man in heaven: and then*
> *shall all the tribes of the earth mourn, and they shall*
> *see the Son of man coming in the clouds of heaven with*
> *power and great glory. (Matthew 24:29-30)*

Over five hundred years earlier, the prophet Daniel saw Christ's second coming in a vision. He said:

> *I saw in the night visions, and behold, one like the*
> *Son of man came with the clouds of heaven, and came*
> *to the Ancient of days, and they brought him near*
> *before him. And there was given him dominion, and*
> *glory, and a kingdom, that all people, nations, and*
> *languages should serve him. (Daniel 7:13-14)*

John said that at Christ's Second Coming every eye would see Him, including those who pierced Him. He said that all the nations of the earth would wail because of Him. This will be a fulfillment of the prophecy given through the prophet Zechariah:

> *And they shall look upon me whom they have*
> *pierced, and they shall mourn for him, as one*
> *mourneth for his only son, and shall be in bitterness for*
> *his firstborn. (Zechariah 12:10)*

The Jews, who have rejected Christ and refused to accept Him as their Messiah, will then see that Jesus is truly the Messiah. For all those who have rejected His Word, it will be a time of fear, despair, and terror. People will run to hide in the mountains and caves and they will cry out:

> *Fall on us and hide us from the face of him that*
> *sitteth upon the throne, and from the wrath of the*
> *Lamb! (Revelation 6:16)*

At Christ's Second Coming, He will gather His Bride to Himself and reward the faithful, but as we will learn further on in our study He will also bring judgment upon the wicked and will tread *"the winepress of the fierceness and wrath of Almighty God"* (Revelation 19:15).

Beloved, this is why it is important for us to be ready! This is why we must have an urgency within our spirits to warn those who continue to reject Christ and His Word. Once Christ returns to this earth, there will be no more time for repentance!

THE ALPHA AND OMEGA

Following the words of greeting and encouragement to the churches, John explained how he received his vision:

> I am Alpha and Omega, the beginning and the ending, saith the Lord, which is, and which was, and which is to come, the Almighty. I John, who also am your brother, and companion in tribulation, and in the kingdom and patience of Jesus Christ, was in the isle that is called Patmos, for the word of God, and for the testimony of Jesus Christ. I was in the Spirit on the Lord's day, and heard behind me a great voice, as of a trumpet, Saying, I am Alpha and Omega, the first and the last: and, What thou seest, write in a book, and send it unto the seven churches which are in Asia; unto Ephesus, and unto Smyrna, and unto Pergamos, and unto Thyatira, and unto Sardis, and unto Philadelphia, and unto Laodicea. (Revelation 1:8-11)

John identifies with the suffering believers by referring to himself as their "brother, and companion in tribulation," then he describes the place where he received the Revelation – exiled and alone on the Isle of Patmos.

Can't you just visualize John standing there on the Lord's Day – alone, forsaken, cold, and weary? The sound of the howling wind echoes through the rocky mountains. The waves crash upon the deserted jagged shoreline...

...But as John begins to worship God, something supernatural occurs. Suddenly, he hears a voice behind him as loud and clear as a trumpet declaring, "...I am Alpha and Omega, the first and the last!" Alpha and Omega are the first and last letters of the Greek alphabet. Christ was describing Himself as being the eternal, complete, revelation of God and He was commanding John to write what he would see in a book to be preserved for the Church.

When John turned to see the source of the mighty voice making this declaration, Jesus Christ – in all His power and glory – was unveiled before his eyes. John saw into the realm of the Spirit and he was so overcome at Christ's awesome presence that he was fearful and fell at His feet as though he were dead!

Along with Peter and James, John had previously received a glimpse of Christ's glory when He was transfigured (Matthew 17:1-8). John had seen Christ's face shine as the sun and His raiment white as the light. But now, John saw Jesus in the fullness of His glory and it was totally overwhelming:

Christ was wearing the robe of the High Priest (verse 13).

John states He was *"clothed with a garment down to the foot, and girt about the paps with a golden girdle."* In the Old Testament, the high priests wore full-length robes with a girdle made of fine linen, embroidered with needlework, secured around their waists. In this vision, Christ had on the robe of a high priest, but the girdle He wore around His chest was made of gold, which denotes the dignity of an important office and signifies His office as our Great High Priest:

> *But this man, because he continueth ever, hath an unchangeable priesthood. Wherefore he is able also to save them to the uttermost that come unto God by him, seeing he ever liveth to make intercession for them. (Hebrews 7:24-25)*

Christ's hair was white like wool (verse 14). Christ's white hair is symbolic of His title – the Alpha and Omega, the first and the last. Christ is eternal, from everlasting to everlasting.

When the prophet Daniel had a similar vision, he also described Him as having hair *"like pure wool,"* raiment *"white as snow,"* and eyes *"as a flame of fire."* (Daniel 7:9-14)

Christ's eyes were as a flame of fire (verse 14). This description is also found in Revelation 19:11-12 where Christ is pictured as a judge and Conqueror over the Antichrist and the nations of the earth who have gathered together for the Battle of Armageddon. His eyes of fire symbolize perfect discernment.

Christ's feet were "like unto fine brass" (verse 15). Brass – a strong, purified metal which results from intense heat – denotes the purity and power with which Christ will bring judgment upon the ungodly of the earth.

Christ's voice was "as the sound of many waters" (verse 15). The voice John first heard in his vision was described as *"a great voice, as the sound of a trumpet,"* loud and clear.

In this verse, John describes Christ's voice as *"the sound of many waters"* which is similar to the description given by the prophet in Ezekiel 43:2. His voice is a mighty, powerful force.

Out of Christ's mouth proceeded "a two-edged sword" (verse 16). This sword represents the power and authority of Christ's words by which the world will be judged (Revelation 19:15)and those aligned with Satan and the Antichrist will be defeated.

Christ's countenance was "as the sun shineth in his strength" (verse 16). The powerful light surrounding Christ was so blinding that John compared it to the powerful rays of the sun in all its strength. In 2 Thessalonians 2:8, Paul tells us that Christ will destroy the Antichrist with the brightness of His coming. Later on in the Book of Revelation (chapter 22), John tells us that in the New Jerusalem there will be no need of the sun, for the Lord God will be our light.

John was totally overwhelmed by this vision of Jesus. I know exactly how he felt. How well I remember the day God took me up into the heavens as a young boy of fourteen years of age. What I saw there overwhelmed me! The manifested glory of God was like a thousand suns and moons all in one! Even today, I still have great difficulty describing the glorious sights I saw and the things I experienced.

Beloved, let me pause right here and ask you: How do you see Christ? Do you see Him as a babe in the manger? Do you see Him only as He was when He lived upon the earth two thousand years ago? Or do you see Him as He really is today...seated in power and majesty at His Father's side?

You may have heard about Jesus all your life. You may even be saved and filled with the Holy Spirit, but have you really received a revelation of Him – "a drawing away of the veil of darkness" – to see Christ as He really is?

How do you see Christ?

FEAR NOT!

John had never seen Jesus like this. He was so overcome with the vision of Christ that he...

> *...fell at his feet as dead. And he laid his right hand upon me, saying unto me, Fear not; I am the first and the last: I am he that liveth, and was dead; and, behold, I am alive for evermore, Amen; and have the keys of hell and of death. (Revelation 1:17-18)*

When you really catch a vision of Jesus, you, too, will be totally overwhelmed – when you really understand His awesome power and majesty!

God's message to you today, is the same as it was to His Apostle John: FEAR NOT! The same message the angel gave to Mary at the annunciation: FEAR NOT! The phrase "fear not" is used over eighty times in the Bible and generally it is to quiet the fears of man in God's Presence.

God is also saying to you today – as He did to John – do not fear your desperate circumstances. Do not fear the future. The One who was dead but is now alive is standing right by your side! There is nothing to fear because Jesus has conquered death and hell. He has power and authority over them. He has absolute power and authority and He wants you to see Him as he really is...high and lifted up, exalted above all things in heaven and on earth.

When you face sickness, disappointments, heartaches, financial problems, and family problems do you see Christ standing beside you as the Great High Priest making intercession for you? Do you see the Mighty Conqueror of death and hell standing ready to give you the victory?

Many believers are living in defeat because their vision of Christ is limited to their natural minds. God wants to take you beyond the limitations of your natural mind so that you may see Him as He is and really know Him in the fullness of His manifested power.

The Apostle Paul prayed that the Ephesians would receive *"a spirit of wisdom and revelation in the knowledge of him"* (Ephesians 1:17). Paul was not talking about head knowledge, but a revelation deep within their spirits.

Jesus Christ, in His glorified state of majesty and power, is depicted as standing in the midst of His Church:

> *The mystery of the seven stars which thou sawest*
> *in my right hand, and the seven golden candlesticks.*
> *The seven stars are the angels of the seven churches:*
> *and the seven candlesticks which thou sawest are the*
> *seven churches. (Revelation 1:18-20)*

The seven candlesticks represent the seven churches in Asia and the stars in Christ's hand represent the angels of the seven churches. It is commonly believed that the angels referred to here are not heavenly beings, but are representative of the pastors and ministers who had authority over the various churches. (In the next book in this series I will explain more about these churches, the conditions that existed at the time, the importance of the messages Christ gave them and how they apply to us).

My prayer for you is that before you finish this prophetic series you will receive a new revelation deep within your spirit of the glorified Christ. You will see Him as He is – standing as a conqueror in the midst of His Church.

It is only when you see Jesus with your spiritual eyes as He is today, that you will see yourself as John did – as a king and priest unto God (Revelation 1:6).

Only when you really see Christ as He is will you be able to overcome the enemy and rise up in power to take your rightful position of authority and dominion upon the earth!

THE OUTLINE OF THE REVELATION

John is commanded to:

> *Write the things which thou hast seen, and the things which are, and the things which shall be hereafter. (Revelation 1:18)*

There are three major divisions in the message contained in this Revelation that Christ gave to John. Christ told John...

1. **To write the things which were: The things he saw, all that was revealed to him through the different visions.**

2. **To write the things which are: Referring to the condition of the churches in Asia Minor at the time.**

3. **To write concerning the things which were to come: The events which would happen in the future as God fulfilled His end-time plan. The literal translation of Revelation 4:1 reads "things which must be after these things" – meaning that the things of Revelation chapters 4-22 must be fulfilled after the "things" revealed pertaining to the churches in Revelation chapters 2-3.**

4. **These three divisions provide an important spiritual key to unlocking the meaning of the Book of Revelation. It is the major outline of all that follows and will provide the broad framework for our future studies.**

Here is a simple outline of the Book of Revelation based on this structure:

An Introduction To Revelation 1:1-21

I. Opening: 1:1-3
   A. It is the revelation of Jesus Christ: 1:1
   B. Purpose: To show things which must shortly come to pass: 1:1
   C. The chain of transmission: 1:1-2
   D. A blessing is given upon those who read, hear, and keep it: 1:3

II. Salutation: 1:4-7
   A. What Christ has done: 1:5-6:
      1. He died for us.
      2. Washed us from our sins.
      3. Made us kings and priests unto God.
   B. What Christ will do: 1:7
   C. Who Christ is: 1:8

III. The theme of Revelation: 1:8

IV. The author: John 1:9-10

V. John's vision of the Lord: 1:10-18
   A. His person: 1:11
   B. His position: In the midst of the churches: 1:12-13
   C. His presence: 1:13-16
      1. Full length garment.
      2. Breastplate of gold.
      3. White hair.
      4. Eyes of fire.

5. Feet of brass.

6. Voice of any waters.

7. Seven stars in right hand.

8 Two edged sword.

9. Shining countenance.

D. John's response: 1:17

E. The message: 1:17

MESSAGES TO THE CHURCHES: 2:1-3:22

I. The message to Ephesus: 2:1-7

II. The message to Smyrna: 2:8-11

III. The message to Pergamos: 2:12-17

IV. The message to Thyatira: 2:18-29

V. The message to Sardis: 3:1-6

VI. The message to Philadelphia: 3:7-15

VII. The message to Laodicea: 3:14-22

REVELATION 4:1-22:21

I. The control of events in the end time: 4:1-5:14

A. The Throne of God: 4:1-11

B. The Scroll: 5:1-5

C. The Lamb: 5:6-14

II. The seven seals: 6:1-8:1

A. The first seal: 6:1-2 The white horse: Conquest

B. The second seal: 6:3-4 Red horse: Blood

C. The third seal: 6:5-6 Black horse: Famine

D. The fourth seal: 6:7-8 Pale horse: Death

E. The fifth seal: 6:9-11 Saints under altar

F. The sixth seal: 6:12-17 Cataclysmic disturbance (An interlude: 7:1-17)
 1. On earth: 7:1-8
 2. In Heaven: 7:9-17
G. The seventh seal: 8:1-11:19 This seal consists of seven trumpets:
 1. First trumpet: 8:7 Hailstorm and fire
 2. Second trumpet: 8:8-9 Volcano
 3. Third trumpet: 8:10-11 Meteor
 4. Fourth trumpet: 8:12-13 Eclipse
 5. Fifth trumpet: 9:1-12 Locusts
 6. Sixth trumpet: 9:13-21 Horsemen
  (An interlude occurs between the sixth and seventh trumpets) Revelation 10:1-11:14
 7. Seventh trumpet: 11:15-19

II. The reign of Satan on earth: 12:1-13:18
A. Satan and Israel: 12:1-17
 1. The woman: 12:1-6
 2. The war in Heaven: 12:7-12
 3. The war on earth: 12:13-17
B. Satan and the world: 13:1-18
 1. The leopard beast: 13:1-10
 2. The two-horned beast: 13:11-14
 3. The conflict with the beast: 13:15-14:20
  (a) Triumph of the 144,000 over the beast, its image, and mark: 14:1-5
  (b) The Lamb and the 144,000: 14:1-5
  (c) Proclamation of three angels: 14:6-13
  (d) The grapes of wrath: 14:14-20

IV. Events preceding the vial judgments: 15:1-8

V. The seven vial judgments: 16:1-21

    A. First vial judgment: 16:2 Sores

    B. Second vial judgment: 16:3 Sea turns to blood

    C. Third vial judgment: 16:4-7 Rivers, springs blood

    D. Fourth vial judgment: 16:8-9 Men scorched by sun

    E. Fifth vial judgment: 16:10-11 Pain and darkness

    F. Sixth vial judgment: 16:12-16 Euphrates dried up; Gather for war

    G. Seventh vial judgment: 16:17-21 Earthquake

VI. Destruction of the world's religious systems: 17:1-18

    A. The scarlet woman and the scarlet beast: 17:1-6

    B. The mystery explained: 17:7-18

VII. Destruction of the world's political and economic systems: 18:1-24

VIII. Defeat of the enemies of God at Armageddon: 19:1-21

    A. The celebration in Heaven: 19:1-10

    B. The confrontation on earth: 19:11-21

        1. Christ the victorious warrior and King of kings: 19:11-16

        2. The beast, his armies, and the false prophet are defeated: 19:17-21

IX. The judgment: 20:4-15

    A. On Satan: 20:1-3,10

    B. Judgment unto life: 20:4-6

    C. The Millennium: 20:6-10

    D. Satan released to deceive the nations once more but is finally defeated: 20:7-10

    E. Judgment unto death: 20:11-15

X. The new heaven and new earth: 21:1-22:5

    A. Introductory overview: 21:1-8

    B. The New Jerusalem in detail: 21:9-22:5

XI. Closing exhortations: 22:6-21

    A. The time is near, do not seal the book: 22:6-11

    B. The testimony of Jesus, The Spirit, and the bride: 22:12-17

    C. Warning and closing prayers: 22:18-21

AN OPEN REVELATION

The Book of Daniel was a sealed book (Daniel 1:9). This meant that everything about the future was not to be revealed at that time. Revelation is an unsealed book (Revelation 22:10). It was written to complete the revelation of God's plan to man.

SYMBOLS IN THE BOOK OF REVELATION

Many people question why God used symbols in the Book of Revelation. Why didn't He just put everything He had to say in plain words?

The answer to this question is multi-faceted. First of all, the style used in Revelation is an example of what is called "apocalyptic literature" which was quite popular from 200 B.C. to 200 A.D. It was a style that was well known and understood by both Jews and Gentiles in the first century Church. A major feature of apocalyptic literature was the use of symbols. Our difficulty in understanding this book is due to our unfamiliarity with apocalyptic literature as a method of communicating a message. The book is also far removed from the historical and cultural context of the times which would make the symbolism easier to understand. That is why to properly interpret it, we must try to understand the historical context in which it was written and interpret it in a manner that would have been meaningful to those to whom it was first addressed.

Second, when Jesus was on earth He often taught by means of parables. The apostles questioned him once concerning this and Jesus explained:

> He answered and said unto them, Because it is given unto you to know the mysteries of the kingdom of heaven, but to them it is not given. For whosoever hath, to him shall be given, and he shall have more abundance: but whosoever hath not, from him shall be taken away even that he hath. Therefore speak I to them in parables: because they seeing see not; and hearing they hear not, neither do they understand. And in them is fulfilled the prophecy of Esaias, which saith, By hearing ye shall hear, and shall not understand; and seeing ye shall see, and shall not perceive: For this people's heart is waxed gross, and their ears are dull of hearing, and their eyes they have closed; lest at any time they should see with their eyes, and hear with their ears, and should understand with their heart, and should be converted, and I should heal them. (Matthew 13:11-15)

The mysteries of God are revealed through parables and symbols to His children, to those who hear with a spiritual ear. They are withheld from the so-called "wise and prudent" (Matthew 11:25).

The rule for understanding symbols in Revelation is simple: Whenever a symbol is used, we look elsewhere in the Bible to learn what that symbol means. For example, in Revelation 1 the vision of Christ in the midst of seven candlesticks is interpreted in verse 20.

SIX SIMPLE RULES FOR INTERPRETING BIBLICAL PROPHECY

1. Study prophecy "in the Spirit," not with natural reasoning.
2. Accept that prophecy can be understood just as it is written without changes or additions by man.
3. Accept the meaning of the words as literal unless the text clearly indicates otherwise. Do not change the literal meaning to spiritual or symbolic meanings. Do not seek to find hidden meanings.

4. Always keep in mind the times and circumstances under which the prophet recorded God's message. Without a knowledge of the historical background, expressions of His time may seem peculiar or difficult to understand.

5. Remember that sometimes prophets describe future events as if they were continuous and successive, but the fact is that there may be thousands of years between. This is sometimes called "the law of prophetic perspective."

6. Keep in mind the "law of double reference." In some passages, two distinct meanings are indicated. For example, In Isaiah 14:4-27 and Ezekiel 28:11-19 the kings of Babylon and Tyre are addressed but these passages also reference the fall of Satan from heaven.

Be sure to obtain your copy of the next book in this powerful new millennium prophecy series, *A Message To The Seven Churches* (Revelation chapters 2-3). Although these messages were written to specific churches in Asia, the same strengths and weaknesses can also be found within the Body of Christ today. In it you will learn strategies for guarding against end-time dangers represented by the seven churches of Asia:

The church at Ephesus: The danger of diminishing love.
The church at Smyrna: The danger of fearing suffering.
The church at Pergamos: The danger of doctrinal compromise.
The church at Thyatira: The danger of moral compromise.
The church at Sardis: The danger of spiritual death.
The church at Philadelphia: The danger of failing to advance.
The church at Laodicea: The danger of lukewarmness.

Morris Cerullo World Evangelism
U.S.: P.O. Box 85277 • San Diego, CA 92186-5277
Canada: P.O.: Box 3600 • Concord, Ontario L4K 1B
U.K.: P.O. Box 277 • Hemel Hempstead, Herts HP2 7D
Email: morriscerullo@mcwe.com
Website: www.mcwe.com